Redemption

§

Lee Passarella

FUTURECYCLE PRESS
www.futurecycle.org

Copyright © 2014 Lee Passarella
All Rights Reserved

Published by FutureCycle Press
Hayesville, North Carolina, USA

ISBN 978-1-938853-35-7

For Candace,
who knows that her redeemer lives

Contents

Living in the Museum § 9

Beasts in Their Jungles 11
Cold Snap, Ides of March 12
Poetry and Murder 13
Old Husbands' Tale 14
Pavlov's, Down by the Log Dump 15
Incorruption 16
From *The Book of the Dead* 17
Memorial 18
Rara Avis 20
Heaven 22
Dia de los Muertos (Day of the Dead) 24
Living in the Museum 25
L'art pour l'art 26
Tropical Depression 27
Brass Rubbing 28
Augury 30
Call of the Wild 31
All Global Warming Is Local 32
Song and Dance: Writing Beethoven's Seventh 34
My Churchyard 36
There's a Divinity 37

Comic Relief § 39

Two Tales Told Out of School: 1. Joe and PW 41
Two Tales Told Out of School: 2. The Dead Go Fast 43
Too Much 47

Redemption § 49

Memento Mori 51
The Truth about Myths 52
Dante's Confession 54

Pilate's Epistle to the Romans...55
A Matter of Perspective (II)..56
Requiescat..57
Cloudscape with Heron..58
The Afterlife...59
Relativity Theory... 60
Civil Rights.. 62
The Time Machine... 65
Jardin des Muses..66
Psalm.. 68
Bethlehem.. 70
Selective Memory.. 72
Kite Flying at Brigantine..74
The Needlefish... 75
Wild Turkeys near Robertstown.. 76
Instinct..77
Sight-Reading Schumann's "The Prophet Bird"......................................78

Notes § 81

Acknowledgments § 91

At length I heard a ragged noise and mirth
　　Of thieves and murderers....

　　George Herbert, "Redemption"

Living in the Museum

Truly, she makes a very good report o' the worm; but he that will believe all that they say, shall never be saved by half that they do: but this is most fallible, the worm's an odd worm.

Antony and Cleopatra, V.ii

Beasts in Their Jungles

The pines groaned all last night,
staggered by an unseen weight
fretting old, parched joints.

Fur of our Shih tzu
as I walk her frames her wise face
in a gust-blown ruff.

She jumps at the skirr
of ghostleaves on macadam,
bobs her head—hangdog,

listening for the thrash of limbs
as the beast that stalks us
shoulders aside the undergrowth.

I come away pitying her
animal terror: I see *myself*
as I slink in, at cold first light,

hunched at the entryway
to waking, salving
last night's ancient wounds.

Cold Snap, Ides of March

We call it a *snap*. But just ask
    the daffodils, their crowns on end:

tiaras of mud and cut glass.
    The velvet calyx gripped in tweezers

like a dead moth to be mounted,
    the tough hose of the stalks

thrust over, crimped shut.
    Stricken fingers point in shocked

recrimination at the sky,
    its icy, distant single star.

Poetry and Murder

Wopsononock Mountain, Western Pennsylvania

Years ago, the lost boy
was found there, a bleached razor,
a fanion of bone that somebody
just happened to glimpse
among the thick laminar of dust
and rust that coats the slope. What he'd
sensed, or suffered, before they found him,
I hadn't heard. Even journalism
draws the line between what we know

and guess. But any February,
the place seems capable of murder
or of poetry: the top congealed
in off-whitecaps, the underparts
sunken, airless. At the base, the city's
flotsam bobs to the top in a trough
between these Allegheny peaks
where the sun scavenges, considering
a tin/gold roof, the priceless bezel
of a windowpane, then turns its Cyclops
eye toward a slope that's dressed
in cloudy harlequin: the fierce gray
panicles of ashes, oaks, and tulip trees
swimming across the surface,
drowned in undertow.

Like the flocced sea a mile out
from shore, a place as gorgeous,
terrible, and unreclaimed
as any in the mind.

Old Husbands' Tale

My long-dead mother would have called it
omen. Each morning between 7 and 9,
the phoebe returns, white moon of her breast
pressed up against the triangle of glass
just below our bedroom ceiling.
A mad clatter at the window, the rusty wings
wigwagging their warning, orange cone
of her beak telegraphing its warning. Or summons.
The beaded yellow feet scrabble
for a way into our warm
conjugal bunker.

Which of us have you come for
then, small oracle,
avenging angel?
Most mornings, I'd rather
it be me.

Pavlov's, Down by the Log Dump

A front yard so full of plastic
things, it couldn't hold two more:
toys & bookshelves, store displays,

cups & plates & pairs of those gummy
children's shoes that look like an insult,
a cutting remark. What wood there is —

the house itself, a buckled picnic table
& its single bench — allegorizes the local
weather, the high-cloud homeliness

overhead. But *you* supply the irony
to this scene: the acres of just-cut pine
in the mucky space next door, strapped

to truck beds, piled in orange stacks
like No. 2 pencils before a test; &
the ancient hound — half St. Bernard? —

hunkered down at one end of the flayed
table, drooling in conditioned response
to some inaudible final bell.

Incorruption

> *The dead do not want us dead....*
> *— Jane Hirshfield*

This photo of skeletal remains
on the Wilderness Battlefield,
May of 1864, could be a friendly monitory,
a Jolly Roger hoisted as a caution to the landlocked
and the deadlocked, to the foot soldier
who is the blood and sinew of any war:
the crossed long bones, the interrogatory skull
complete with mock furrow to its brow
(though incomplete as to the grinning mandible).

It might, in small, be the vision
of a bombed-out city from our own century.
Here, the vacant eyeholes of houses
stare back at us, the broken arches of busy bridges
no longer busy, and bridging nowhere.

Over there, the flying buttress
of the pelvic bone buttresses its nothing,
the cathedral a ruin, the master builder
in comfortable retirement somewhere
where the dead leaves don't pile up on the lawn,
winter after winter.

From *The Book of the Dead*

The world of the coroner
is well lighted as underworlds go,
but as monochrome
as a catafalque, a winding-sheet—
some appurtenance of the dead. Gurneys,
tables, sinks, lockers, scales: everything
chrome steel, endless steel.

He is the great god Anubis of the place,
judge of the dead.
He has no use for the ankh,
the key to a human life. It is the key
to nothing that he needs to know.

But like Anubis, he weighs the heart.
His *Physicians' Desk Reference* says,
*The human heart weighs between 250
and 400 grams and is the size of a clenched fist....*

...he weighs the homeboy's heart
and the apoplectic merchant's heart
and the pimp's heart;
he weighs the jaundiced bag lady's heart.

He weighs the raped and beaten
and cut-up housewife's heart:
318 grams, it says. *This heart is true.*

Memorial

World War II Memorial opens on National Mall
— News item, April 30, 2004

My Uncle Jack missed by twenty years
seeing a memorial sixty years in the making.
Maybe he would have felt it was his due,
like the free drinks he cadged
back in the '40s, a newly wounded vet.

In those days he made this joke:
"If they tell me 'Just drop your right eye
in the till,' I got 'em there!" Uncle Sam
gave him a glass eye to replace
the good one he lost in Yugoslavia in '44,
after two years slogging through North Africa,
up the boot of Italy. My mother told me
his men broke down and cried when he got hit.

Later, though, the most you could get out of him
was a grin and change of subject.
Bloodthirsty as kids are, I once asked,
"Uncle Jack, did you kill a lot of Germans?"
"Literally thousands!" he answered, beaming.
And that was all. *Nice weather, if it don't rain.*

What I heard about his tour came secondhand.
The Silver Star that should have been
a Medal of Honor, the lieutenancy he passed up.
"Sarge" was a good enough handle for him.
Once, Mom told me about the time
his company took out a machinegun nest.

Among the "thousands" of Germans
that he'd killed were the boys he saw
lying there as if asleep: blond, clean-cut,
hard-bodied as quarterbacks. They weren't the Enemy
that day. Just sons and brothers.
And a kind of beauty you didn't learn about
in boot camp. That day, his famed right eye
did what glass can't ever.

Rara Avis

Carmansville, New York, summer 1850

Eleven a.m. The family rises severally
from its fifth meal of the day. John James
taking his fare now as the birds do — ten, eleven,
twelve meals — with busy, flustering calls
and gestures, the other Audubons
always in bemused and reluctant attendance.

Just before twelve and the day's sixth meal,
Lucy appears at the study door, in old, crushed
green taffeta, as rumpled and as fragile as the lichen
in her husband's famous painting of the Ivory Bills,
her eyes weary ciphers behind the spectacles' glare.
With her, a well-dressed traveler in tailcoat
and white waistcoat, yellow stirrup pants
looping the soles of riding boots, *A very goldfinch
of a man,* John James would have said in another life.
The stranger bears his favorite plate from the Royal Octavo,
1843, the Long-billed Curlews: a soft geometry
of curve on curve on curve, the male's bill
curving to his crustacean dinner in the sand,
the female's curved above his sloping back,
sinuous neck craned rearward, fixing us with a quizzical
and guarded stare. A November sky torn gently
here and there to let the blue light in. Across the harbor,
tiny Charleston, steeple-peaked, and farther still,
the thin pink benison of sunset, Man and his systems
a distant pair of irrelevances in this bird's-eye view.

A kind enthusiast, the stranger compliments
the master, his mouth ajar in half-smiling anticipation.
John James stares blankly back.
                              After minutes, the lips
move, and move again. Then the words come,
a hard birth: *Ah, yes. Beautiful. Two daughters.*
Both gone now. Too sweet for this old world,
we like to say. Too sweet.
                    And nothing more.

Noon passes, the family relieved to postpone
that looked-for sixth meal of the day.
John Woodhouse's two young daughters
hurry with their books and snacks wrapped
in kerchiefs down to the sun-sheathed Hudson,
rushing for its appointment with the Atlantic
twenty miles away. But John James is lost
now somewhere along the snaky Ohio,
in the twilit purlieus of the Ivory Bill,
the Passenger Pigeon: the soon-extinct.

Heaven

When you broke your hip
it was as if someone had said
*He's used to it. He can take a little
more.* Then, when I saw you afterward,
you had become someone I hardly knew,
let alone loved. Someone I would read
about in the paper, who had died
of "an extended illness." How *did*
you put up with it? The PT when you
could barely stand? And all the words
and pills they fed you, for everything except
the infection that would kill you in a single day?

Your death certificate reads like Beethoven's,
with his tragicomic half-dozen ills —
it was a race you didn't run yourself,
where sepsis pneumonia leukocytosis
won placed and showed.

And then the funeral: the undertaker hoped
we hadn't seen too much, how the grave
diggers sealed your casket in the vault,
the clever rig on their backhoe
traversing what had become of you
like the cool uncalculated
movements of a croupier's hands,
or the career Catholic
making the autonomic Sign.

Now, as I see it all through that film
of piety, that metaphysical tear
we spot ourselves when the edges
get too sharp, I don't imagine
a cloud of wings, the white vesture,
and the forever sun. Instead, I see
the smallest comforts: the dried tear,
the embrace of darkness, the rest
from the endless casting of the lots.
And I grasp at it as if that's all
I ever want of heaven.

Dia de los Muertos (Day of the Dead)

Dear Mom and Dad,

If I thought that you'd come back to me—
if only for a visit—I'd offer you much more
than this day's traditional *atole,*
pan de muerte: corn gruel.
Sauerkraut with slabs of grease-slick pork
and noodles rich with stroke-inducing stew beef—
any of that heady and caloric stuff
we'd have on special days.
For this is one.

I'd top it off with beet-red Jello
enveloping a No. 2 can-full of shimmering
fruit cocktail, piled high with Redi-Whip.
Two steaming cups of percolator coffee
and Cremora. A meal fit for the Eisenhowers
I would offer you.

Now, Mom and Dad, curl up
on these two quaint *petates* I've laid down here
just for you, and tell me why, and if,

Lazarus ever laughed.

Living in the Museum

I awoke on the gray
shelf of a reef, looking
up at a surface the color
of old snapshots,
or the undersides of waves.
The first leaning drops
turned the window to cut
glass. I wanted to put it
in a showcase.

Then the waves broke
over it. The runoff
trailed like arteries,
in beating knots, every
twisted thing I saw
trapped in amber,

in the lens at the bottom
of the bottle.

The house wore that window
all day long
like a locket.
An amulet.

L'art pour l'art

> *It is good that war is so terrible, else we would come to love it too much.*
> *— Robert E. Lee at the Battle of Fredericksburg*

Sometimes, the tale tells *you*. Take the story
of St. Julian the Hospitaller by Flaubert. It's one of sin
and redemption, of beautiful redemption and even more
beautiful sin beautifully, brilliantly, sensuously rendered.
It does for cruelty to animals what *Apocalypse Now* did for war.
Invites us to hate the sinner, but leaves us with this terrible
hankering for the sin.
                        The smell of fresh beasts' blood
is Julian's Napalm in the Morning: a woodcock cut off
at the feet as it sits its frozen branch, cranes whip-cracked dead
on the fly, out of thin air. Heaps of dying stags spew bright blood
at one end, bowels at the other. Julian uses hatchets on the wolves,
knives on the bears, spears on wild boars. He's never met
a sharp object that he doesn't love.
                      A pigeon that refuses
to die is so hateful he strangles it, high on the sensuality of gore
like a teenager fucking himself black & blue. Horror is made
pristine, with the sleek exactitude of a murderer honing his craft,
polishing the text of his MO like a résumé. When Julian
finally kills his parents, there's no terror in the act. It seems
like perfect logic after all that other blood.

When we first read *Madame Bovary*, we feel for the heroine
so much we're surprised to learn Flaubert wrote the book
to kill off that Bovary in himself, that preening sentimentalist
lurking in his own bourgeois heart. What in himself
did he hope St. Julian would kill off?
And why did he come to love the killing so?

Tropical Depression

Rain. The sea grapes rasp
in their brittle throats,
sounding the day's death rattle.
The sun knifes through, in one last
vindictive slash. Clouds weep red. A film
of it adheres to every wave, until this bloody
day climbs inside you, a virus hunting for
the likeliest victims, getting so tangled up in you
you can't tell what is You
and what is It.

Like a House of Usher: neurasthenic Rod,
his pissed-off sister tangled in their lovedeath
at the end of the story. But this story
doesn't end. It just drags on
with the same old props—night trailing
its sheets of rain, and next,
the gray ghost at the window
bringing stale news
of some impending
wreck.

Brass Rubbing

When my nails-tough mother found out
she'd bear another child at 38,
16 years after her last one, she shared
an endearment with hard-working Dad:
"You son of a bitch!" This,
my father (who outlived her by almost 20 years)
never shared with me, but I heard about it anyway—
too rich a confidence for my wife,
his last years' confidant, to keep under wraps.

As a child, I always grieved
to think my cousins could have been my aunts,
that my parents were as old as the grandparents
of my friends and my detractors.
When I learned about the "mistakes"
that couples make sometimes, I naturally assumed
I was one. But finally, to give my life the gloss
that lets us live, I told anyone who cared
I wasn't a mistake—I was balm for their old age.
And they *did* love me like their skins,
and even better. Fathoms deeper
than they loved each other, Mom with her holy rages,
her three-day silent treatments.

Having come to them in the fall
of their infrequent fruiting, I lost my parents young.
So now—Mom dead these 30 years—
I can choose to see them mostly
through the diffusion lens of a selective memory,

or in a kind of bas-relief, a noble bit
of funerary art: Here lies the Lord,
there, his obeisant Lady. I rub the brass,
translate their images, create of them an icon
of paper and of wax. A history
unponderous as a kite aloft.

Augury

As I drive to work, two vultures
sit on the shoulder of the road
picking through trash, solemn and unruffled
as bag ladies, the gray drapery of their feathers
tented over their humped asses
like outsized raincoats.

I want them to be dreadful:
slag-gray wings spreading to the very corners
of the frame my car window makes
out of this scene on the icy verges
of an old man's bleared Thanksgiving—
invalid wife sicker still today,
sinuses rotten with infection;
my hangover lifting its gray scrim
above the mediocrity of a job suffered
only by degrees: Oil spill. Melanoma.
Soul's eclipse.

But there they sit, wings folded back
into two brief hunches
at the shoulder. No grim majesty
anywhere to be seen. Bodies sketchy,
shapeless—huge barnyard hens
with heads the gravelly white

of decayed snow melting
down into rumpled wattles.
Omens not of death
but worse. Of life.

Call of the Wild

Hot July, in a valley of the Shadow:
a hill once packed with pine and oak
tight as a pile of cordwood, gone

to make my company's new office park
—the Campus, as it's jocularly called,
this Cadmus' field of macadam and tinder

grass. Behind the place, from a dying
tulip tree—forest leftover, anorexic slip
all raw long bones and hip blades tottering

above ten lanes of Interstate—a red hawk
calls its mate half a mile away. A mournful
cloying *cheecheechee:* crazy mismatch

to the bulk of this tented *thing* that lurches
and kites downwind, like a jinni haunting
a spot where death is a dream of shade....

This week, we filled the swimming pool
at home, our tiny garden by the backdoor
ankle-deep with the overflow. Each hot

parched night we hear the frogs
croon love songs in the brief wetland
formed from our profligate days.

All Global Warming Is Local

1

Early fall. A string of days
at least five degrees above average.
This morning, the wet sidewalks, the webby trees
sheathed in wet lamplight should be as welcome
as that first birdcall from the jaundiced
dogwood in the neighbor's front yard.
Instead, it's a vinegar sop.
With a chaser of wormwood.

As I walk them, the dogs nose
the dank wind like a stranger. And it is,
in this year of the 100 Years' Drought.
The air smells oddly of curry,
a vegetable stew of rendered plant life
in the rank pot likker of Georgia humidity.
Overhead, a black sieve throws
holy water on the damned.

2

Seen from the air, Lake Lanier
looks like the Delta, sifting the brown gold
of the Mississippi through its brown fingers.
But Lanier deposits nothing. It's all
withdrawals. The boat docks

are high, dry, unhandsome.
A hundred feet from any water,
ironic surfboards ride strata
of dust. Like the dubious chits
from some marathon poker game
where the dealer has just lost his shirt.

3

Hard of head, in the driveway
the dogs strain at the leash as I stoop
for the newspaper. They're creatures
of short memory, who live in the immediate,
all for the comforts of home
with its treat jar on the counter
and its two full doggie dishes
on the kitchen floor.

I freshen their water dish
for them, carrying it from the sink
like a chalice.

Song and Dance: Writing Beethoven's Seventh

> *Vienna, spring 1812*
> *The Symphony [No. 7 in A major] is the apotheosis of the dance.*
> — *Richard Wagner*

His own head is the cage he's trapped in,
a bird whose song is sung for the sake of others.
As for himself, listening to that song is like looking
at the world through the broad end of a telescope.

He thrashes at the keys of his old Érard only to hear
what is tantamount to the sound made
by a little girl's music box. Stuffed under a cushion.
In the far corner of a room across the hall.

Sometimes, it seems as though the cage of his head
holds nothing more than silence and that endless
ratcheting ache behind his eyes. And in the evening,
the creeping fog of wine, with its brief surcease.

Movement I: Coda. He squints and scribbles out
the gentle galloping line he hears down in the cellos.
His fingers stumble through the thicket of black keys,
fumbling along the bass register *like crazy old Ludwig himself*
shuffling to his slops jar. He chuckles at his own bon mot,
then kicks the jar; a silent slosh of warm piss
wreathes the floorboards under the piano.
That's why I always keep it handy!

The boozy fingers latch onto B sharp,
which is to an A-major chord like vinegar poured
over teacakes. Even in the dead silence

of his cage, he can hear it growling in the cellos
and contrabasses, nipping at the heels of the flutes'
and violins' sunny E, the clarinets' bell-like
held G sharp, the horns' top-of-lungs-ecstatic E over A.

He's quick to jot down B sharp. *Let the damned thing stand,*
he mumbles (or maybe shouts; to him it's all the same).
It is the sound of wine dogging pain and of pain
dogging wine in an endless mocking dance.

My Churchyard

This evening, as I set out
cone flowers, their green stars cool
with the promise of bloom—tiny firmament
on stilts full of rain—the garden's haunted
by spirits as silent and rank
as an undergrowth:

phantom tickseed's bright buttons
undone; blue lupine's ghost spires
dissolved; cotton-candy astilbe,
a specter in pink.

Zeniths white-hot and parched dormancies
—the friendless cruelties of Southern
gardening—have done for them all.
No great gardener, I....

The departed watch with an eyeless intent,
with pity and scorn, the sexton's
dull ministrations. The grim work
of spade and bell rope.

There's a Divinity....

Anton Bruckner plays Hamlet to Beethoven's Yorick, Vienna, 1888

A devout Catholic, he built to praise his God
    huge hulking cathedral-symphonies where
        even the willing listener finally gets lost,

mind wandering among the gray arcades and vaults,
    arches within arches, endlessly on end. *Bruckner*
        has his great moments oh but his dreadful half hours!

For twenty years and more, the critics said
    his symphonies were "wild," "absurd,"
        "unplayable," and helpfully rewrote them

for him. So after a successful performance
    of his Fourth Symphony, he strode beaming
        to the podium, tipped the conductor a *thaler,*

said *Have a beer on me old boy!*
    When they were about to move Beethoven's
        exhumed remains from Währinger Cemetery

to more hallowed quarters in the *Zentralfriedhof,*
    he rushed into the examination chamber,
        brushed aside the flabbergasted doctors

studying the corpse, and took
    the stinking skull in both his hands.
        Searched those blank eye sockets

for the man whose final, 70-minute
    symphony had pointed him the way down
        the long and lonely nave he worshiped in.

Comic Relief

SCENE I. A churchyard.

    Enter two Clowns, with spades, & c

First Clown

    Is she to be buried in Christian burial that wilfully seeks her own salvation?

Second Clown

    I tell thee she is: and therefore make her grave straight: the crowner hath sat on her, and finds it Christian burial.

        Hamlet, V.i

Two Tales Told Out of School:
1. Joe and PW

Genesis 39 explained by one of my World Lit students

I don't know if this story'll
make sense to you, but here goes anyway....
First of all, Potiphar's wife—
we'll call her PW, 'cause the Bible
doesn't get specific—is not
some old witch. No, she's a fine-looking woman,
a little old for Joe, sure, but fine.
It isn't like, man, take your hands off
me, old bitch! I'm outta here! And besides,
it isn't like Joe's got his pick of babes,
either. At least the Bible doesn't mention
any babes except PW, so I'm guessing
Potiphar's dump is out there in the middle of nowhere.
Which most of Egypt was back then anyway.
And Joe's not gay, you know, and he doesn't need
a hit of Viagra or nothing like that. And PW's
got her damn motor running and all....

But, like, it's not like Joe's *afraid*
of what's going to happen if his boss finds out.
I mean, it's not like If her hubby catches us,
I'm dead meat! No. It's more like I owe this guy
something, don't I? He writes the checks,
you know, and here I am cheatin' on his ass
with his old lady! I mean, *no way* does Joe
want Potiphar to get bent out of shape
(and as things turn out, Joe ends up
in the slam anyway, 'cause the bitch does

Lee Passarella § 41

a number on him) but that's *not* why he clears
out of Potiphar's bare-ass naked....

Ah, man, I told you this shit
don't make sense. Just forget it.

Two Tales Told Out of School:
2. The Dead Go Fast

> *A poetic paraphrase, with apologies to Gottfried Bürger*
> *and Dante Gabriel Rossetti*
>   — *for my students*

—PROEM—
But anyway, Bürger's "Ballad of Lenore"
is just like all the rest. It spends a whole lot of time
trying to scare the pants off of you
before tying itself up in moral slipknots.
But it all boils down to that old cliché,
Be careful what you wish for —
you may get it. Here's how the story goes,
and you tell me if I'm all wet....

                 —

Sweet little Lenore's betrothed
to this German knight named Wilhelm,
who's majorly macho. He's the first
on his block to sign up for a tour of duty
in Hungary, where the two sides go at it firetongs
and hammerhandles, with casualties piling up
faster than DUIs on St. Patrick's Day,
till King Frederick and the Empress get bored
and call it quits. Now everybody's happy
as if they'd just invented Jägermeister,
but Willy doesn't make it back to Germany.
As you can guess, Lenore takes it pretty hard,
flops down in tears, yanks at her hair
and everything. Her mother's the voice
of reason. There's more fish in the sea,
she says. In fact, Willy's probably got some

little gypsy girl down in Prague that's more to his liking.
Besides, it's God's will. *Kommt, Liebschen,*
Gott vill brrring you comfort, if you yust play ball mit Him.
Lenore says thanks but no thanks. No *Ave Marias*
for her: Heaven and earth are both a dump,
far as she's concerned. She might as well go
take a flying leap in the grave, now her charming
Willy's gone. Mama's the old-fashioned type,
though, and asks God to forgive her distraught
little daughter's blasphemies. *Ach,* you know
vot kids are like, *Gott,* she says. Lenore's still in a state,
of course, crying her eyes out for her *Schatze,* when —
speak of the devil! that night, who should ride
up to her house like he's just been down
to the corner store for a pack of smokes?
Willy's dressed to kill, still wearing that metal suit
of his, helmet and all. He calls out to her,
Come on, Sugar, open the gate,
and I'll take you away from all this,
to our new bridal bed, which is only
about a 100 miles from here as the crow flies.
My swift steed'll get us there by first light (give or take).
Willy, are you gassed?! Lenore rightly queries.
It's 11 p.m., and *you think* we can get there by sunup?
But, hey, she asked for this, so it would be
kind of churlish not to grab her trail mix
and her Birkenstocks, then climb on board!
So off they go. He tells her all about
the nice little berth they'll share,
which is *cool* and *narrow* and for some reason
has a lid on it (hint), but Lenore is hearing
what she wants to hear at this point,

44 § **Redemption**

daydreaming about the cottage
and the picket fence, you know. Meanwhile,
Willy's still reassuring her about the time.
We and the dead go fast, we and the dead go fast,
he keeps on saying, which, I'm telling you,
would calm the hell out of me!
But Lenore's kind of thick. I mean,
they go past funeral processions and stuff,
and he keeps asking her if she fears "the quiet dead"
(*there's* foreshadowing if I ever saw it),
and all she says is, Me? No way, I'm fine.
I don't know, maybe she's just being polite,
but she finally starts getting nervous
when they pass a gallows and this pack
of loitering ghosties tag along for fun.
Faster and faster the filly careens through the night,
kicking up the scenery like a redneck
laying rubber on a gravel road. All of a sudden,
Willy's jerkin (whatever that is) crumbles
away to nothing, like a fight-scene movie prop,
and my God! he's got no skin on him!
The guy's pure bone, and she notes,
with some trepidation, that he's sporting a scythe
and hourglass, just like You-Know-Who!
Poor Lenore's eyes are big as schnitzels now,
and her hair's standing up straight
as storm troopers on parade! Well,
pretty soon Willy (or whoever the hell he is,
cause Lenore's starting to smell a rat, *big time*)—
anyhow, Willy or whoever's muscling his way
through the churchyard gate, and they go
barreling over a whole bunch of graves

without so much as a by-your-leave.
The "bridal party" — that gaggle of ghouls
who came along for the ride? — they're shrieking
and zooming around like bats out of the proverbial
Home of Batdom, the cock has crowed,
and Willy's faithful nag exits we-know-not-whither.
Though Lenore puts up one hell of a fight,
at last she shuffles off this mortal coil.
The End. And what's the moral of the story?
Your arm's too short to box with God,
so get over it. The dead go fast.
And stay gone, if you're lucky.

Too Much

Villanelle for William

"The world is too much with us," someone said.
(Not sure who, but it doesn't matter now;
whoever the guy was is surely dead).

Sometimes I feel that way: I lie in bed
and think I'd rather kill my eats with bow
and arrow than just get and spend, as said

that someone — not sure who — who thought we're led
to give our hearts away and don't allow
ourselves the time (before we're surely dead)

to stop and watch the moon rise, golden red,
above "This Sea that bares her bosom...." How
a sea can have a bosom, like he said,

is to personify the thing instead
of call a spade a spade, for all time stow
the used-up lingo of the surely dead.

Same thing with "Triton's horn": I'm really fed
up with allusions — deck that sacred cow!
The world was too much with him, like he said,
that guy who's, evidently, long since dead.

Redemption

>   ...there I him espied,
>   Who straight, *Your suit is granted,* said, and died.
>
>   George Herbert, "Redemption"

Memento Mori

i

For the Elizabethans, the act of love
was a death in little.
How they must have cherished death,
to consider that most intimate,
and animate, of acts a practice run for dying.
Death would need to be something realer,
and much more lovely, for us to love it now
as much as that.

ii

From our window, we can see the wreckage
of two barely living maples
at the corner of the motel parking lot.
Long finger bones point at us
through the armature of green. Below,
the cowed trunks are wound with ancient ivy,
as if to hold the dying wood together.

Standing entwined by the window,
our bodies aren't perhaps as young
as they once were, but just as willing —
the bed a sweaty tangle from the lovemaking,
and death, for us, a token unreal
as those dead fingers
lost against the backlit sky.

The Truth about Myths

Shih tzus make excellent mothers, the handbook says,
and she is one, down to tongue-disposing of the very
waste that's dribbled from their nubby little spouts.

Five pups, all males. And when their pre-dawn
scratch and clamber wake us, she jumps up
into the plastic wading pool that is their home-

within-our-home to stop the racket of their paws
and mouths. Night or day, they cry out to her
in the voices of some other species — weird ontogeny.

"The whales!" my wife says, half asleep; then, whales
and their songs it may well be. But litter of piglets,
pack of rats, flock of shorebirds, even, comes to mind.

Finally, their racket becomes our poor dog's pain
objectified: battering ram, siege cannon to the ear,
the heart. On milk alone, they grow from an ounce or two

to a couple pounds, their jaws the powerful siphons
that fuel their always-neediness. They ring her dry
as an orange squeezed down to the pulp, until her belly

sags from her like she's been flayed, the dugs gray,
limp and pendulous as garden slugs hung from leaves.
The rasp of her spine is intricately *there,* underneath

the straitened skin. I think of that myth about the pelican,
how it's presumed to feed its young on the meat
of its own breast— a noble little lie *she* tells me

has more than a crumb of truth. More of truth
than I have in me when, absently, I pat
her head, toss her the ritual bone *Good dog.*

Dante's Confession

After Inferno, *Canto V*

I've heard the fair sex sometimes
feign that sweet paroxysm Eve invented
in the Garden, after she "did eat"
and she'd learned the fleshly arts.

It's a kindly meant deception,
taking into account the way to a man's
heart is really through that huge
and tumid, God-*forsaking* ego of his
(the largest organ he's got about him!),
instead of through a lesser organ, as some report.

Well, it's all a game anyway, Lord help us....

And so it was that I concocted
my gentle little ruse for Francesca's
sake, my girlish sham demise — in short,
my famous swoon:

a tribute meant for her who brought
death into the world and now
would give a world if she could die
down to her soul,

poor child.

Pilate's Epistle to the Romans

Transalpine Gaul, A.D. 36

I'll grant the Emperor this much at least:
even if he wants you dead, it comes
with a certain dignity. I get to choose the time
and place. As long as I don't leave town.
Or take too long about it. My own blade,
my own hand on the hilt. Unless I care
to delegate, have my slave do the thing.
(Which wouldn't be very soldierly of me,
I confess.) So here's to the Emperor.
We who are about to die....

Sorry, by the way, Vitellius,
to have offended our precious colonials,
the Jews, and their grimy little desert God.
I hesitate to say you don't know them
as well as I do, but...you don't know them
as well as I do. I predict that you, or whoever
gets the nod after you, won't be as easy on them
as I was. Won't give them a trial (fair or not—
I know the allegations). Nail them one by one
to the tree. Kill them off slowly. One at a time.
No. You'll kill whole legions of these Messiah-
seeking bastards. Someday. Turn their stinking Temple
into a coliseum. Or a stable.

But then, you can't argue politics
or religion. And who can spare the time?

A Matter of Perspective (II)

Okay. Now take this guy, this Bible-believer, to the Uffizi.
Show him Fra Angelico's *Coronation of the Virgin*.
Point out the pomp and majesty, or just the composition:
the assembled saints in their semicircle, the gorgeous corona
that perfects the circle, envelopes all in scalloped polychrome.
The marvelous anagogy in the seraphim whose trumpets
will one day summon sheep and goats to their division.
At the very center, anchoring the whole, Jesus and *Regina Mundi*,
floating on a cloud like the one He'll ride on Judgment Day.

How would you answer when your guest maintains
That's not in the Bible. Where do you see it in the Bible?
Bring history to bear, bring all the art-historical baggage
you can lug. Then try to see it his way for a moment.
In his eyes, this isn't some wonderfully enlightened vision.
He might even say it's *dark, demonic*. Set that aside for now.
Just look at things the way he sees them. Here's this *painter*
making Jesus crown his mom, the handmaiden, the girl
who didn't even get it when He said "My father's business."
Knock the intellectual underpinnings out from under anything,
you end up with empty gestures, if not just plain bullshit.
See how relativistic stuff like art, culture, civilization are?
I mean, take it out of art history class, it's really kind of cheap
and funny, this so-called masterpiece: Jesus and his mother
ride their flying carpet; He gives her this *crown*
like she's some kind of beauty queen,
while the angels blow their riffs and licks,
and the saints applaud as if she'd saved the world.

Requiescat

> *This wallpaper is killing me; one of us has got to go.*
> — last words of Oscar Wilde

A wan (though beefily substantial) ghost,
he haunted streets that'd feted him before.
He preyed on countrymen who'd heard the lore
about his fall. Yet none presumed to boast
superiority — played gentle host
instead, since the absinthe he favored more and more
was so well recompensed: the endless store
of epigrams and bon mots, all but lost

on poor old proper England now. Still, he
had little luck in Paris streets, as free,
almost, of love for him as London's. So,
when money came — infrequently — he bought
love. Death was just an afterthought, a blow
as slight as his least sin. A minor blot.

Cloudscape with Heron

Twilight clone-gray overhead,
    as though the river cast its image

upwards, hung it from the rafters,
    from the tottering birches and catalpas

where they crisscross. Where the great
    bird threads those twin firmaments: Gray

kite hauled on its ghost-string, halting.
    Gray wraith trailing its winding-sheet.

The Afterlife

> *In Heaven, it is always autumn.*
> *— John Donne, "On the Nativity"*

We've all heard the old saw,
that a broken clock, in its infinite
wrongness, is right two times a day.
But the broken crime scene clock is always
right, forever fixing the stale coordinates
of the act with its two dead hands.
In CSI Heaven, it is perpetually 7:24,
and the crime has always just happened.

In the city park, the broken clocks
sit on familiar benches, taking the sun,
though it doesn't take them.
Nothing, not a glimmer, registers
on those crazed surfaces, those intricately
ruined faces, as the day passes
them by. The wheels refuse to turn
and mesh. Their hands idle in the stark
white space where Time has forever

just ended, and where it is always
still April of '96. July of '03.
Or February of '99.

Relativity Theory

In the wake of Hurricane Katrina
August 30, 2005

For Peggy

Green on green. Redbuds and maples
against the darker pines —
in this high wind and half-light,
a place briefly lovely as a coral reef,
the underwater currents'
many fingers combing the rich
growth west to east, west to east.
To the north, the storm clouds
mate, knotting one another in slick, fat coils,
showing here and there
their near-white underbellies.

That's how it appears
where I sit thinking, at a red light in Atlanta,
on the pinwheeling verges
of the storm. Here, it is an endless,
gorgeous yin and yang.
But along the Gulf, from New Orleans
crabwise to Mobile, it has been
this vastly hungry thing,
self-interested, indifferent
as a boa trussing up a mouse.

For me, it all comes down to this:
Last night, I learned the surgeons ferreted
out the tangled monster that has bred
among the imagined channels

of your fine brain,
making its foul snakes' wedding
in the places I have loved
but never seen. And suddenly, *this*
has become the all of human unhappiness—
this unseen beauty I imagine,
where the blackness bred,
and still breeds, its mandrake-
rooted you-and-not-you.

Civil Rights

It is one of the many summers
of our discontent. August of '59:
the Phillies are a collection of has-beens
and would-bes—Robin Roberts,
Wally Post, Sparky Anderson, Chris Short.
Together, on a steam-heated evening
in Philadelphia, they are far less
than the sum of their parts. Tonight,
the Giants will hand them another
of their 90 losses of the year. In the stands,
a 10-year-old who doesn't know
how really bad they are, though that thick
silence in the air is the white noise
of surly fans and speechless home-team bats.
Nor does he know how really good
the young black man out in center field is.
He's heard of Willie Mays, of course.
But he's indifferent to that magnet of a glove,
that feral bat that can chew up 500 feet
of turf and bleachers like a barracuda
in a school of albacore.   The air is larded
with a cumulative stink: 50 years
of roasted peanuts, steamed red hots.
It's spongy, visible, unfurled like a sodden
roll of gauze beneath the lights of Connie Mack.
Moths as big as house wrens crisscross
the whited space between. Out of the stands,
some guy goes running across the field,
legs pumping like *this* is the wind sprint
that will get him to the majors.

And it is: there, in center field, he stands
before the Kid himself. Sticks out
his small, pale hand, lips forming
Put 'er there! And Willie just stares.
Stares, hands on hips. *Man, you're nuts!*
I'm not shakin' hands with you.
But you have to give it to that tiny
white man out in center field: There he stands,
still proffering his papery little hand,
and Willie still refusing, head
wagging now, schoolmarm fists
on hips.
        Then the guards
are leading the guy across the field,
arms thrust in a *V* above his head, a victory
salute to the wild-about-it crowd.
Later, the 10-year-old would learn the word
ejected. But now, this guy's just getting kicked out,
into the hot dark night of North Broad Street.
On Monday, this fan would share
his bohunk bon mot, his *youshouldaseenit*
tale with the guys over hoagies
and thermoses of coffee on the job
in Fishtown or Passyunk,
wherever it might be. Day after that,
it would be the same old tune all over again:
The goddamn niggers are fuckin' up this town.
Damn blockbusting coons! Move
down the street from you, and you can kiss
the freakin' neighborhood goodbye.

So don't do it, Willy, the 10-year-old thinks
now, almost 50 years gone by.

Don't go gentle.
Don't shake the hand
that would aim the fire hose.
That would sic the dogs.
Don't say "hey" to every fan
in this mad and
twisted and
tragically conflicted crowd.

The Time Machine

i. In the screening room

The redbuds are studded with a blood-red
growth that spreads by the minute,
as if caught in time-lapse photos,
the gray-brown background unchanging

as a snapshot. It's an old picture,
a publicity still. I recognize the people
in it, long-dead film stars whose movies play
each night in my slowly unwinding head.

ii. Le temps, la durée

Because eventually, it happens: you step outside
the frame, beyond the calendar of the lovely
quotidian, where suburbanized nature ticks off
the young weeks — the early cherry and star magnolia,

the flowering quince and ornamental pear,
the dogwood with its alleged stigmata.
Beyond Shrovetide and Easter, to become
that ultimate, unregenerate you.

Jardin des Muses

> *Tho' much is taken, much abides....*
> *— Tennyson, "Ulysses"*

1.

This has been a March
more like June — days in the mid-70s,
the primrose lolling parched
tongues over the mulch at the back of the house.
The first trees to bloom — okames,
star magnolias — caught in the mangle
look limp at close quarters,
the white stars pulpy on the branch,

the pink globes of blossom
grizzled and frayed. Today the world
looks old. But across the road,
against the pale smear of last year's witch
grass, these same dull
trees are improbable paintball splats
of color, a child's artwork.

2.

How we labored over it,
dipping the hunks of sponge in watercolor,
bent to our task like jewelers.
Tamping the butcher paper up
and down with the pink and purple blotches,
calling it spring.

3.

Toward the end, Renoir
painted with the brushes tied
to his fingers, sapped and burled
with pain: Odysseus lashed

to the mast. His need to know
the murdering
sweetness of their song.

Psalm

1.

The sky is writing letters to itself,
bleak missives torn from an endless pad.
They whirl, in black eddies and vortices,
around a door framed in light
that offers sole escape from this house
of cozy self-recrimination the storm has built.
From newel to eaves, and eaves to cornice,
vortices that catch dead scraps of leaves
in a slow, gray dance: cloud on purling
cloud. A fugue and double fugue
of cloud. Then the door opens, unfurls
like a white rose, calyx and petal.

2.

*The Lord made for my lord a footstool
of his enemies.* Of which, O God,
I am the most recalcitrant, the most stiff-necked. Lord,
I am the grubbiest of Thy many footstools.
But above me, a wild sky leaves its tattered past
behind, strewed like old newsprint.

3.

God in three persons: Father, Son,
and Holy Telegraph, Holy Wireless:
a ceaseless dialogue — stars, clouds, sand
harangue each other back and forth
across black chasms.

Forgive me, Father....
...against...Thee only...have I sinned....
...and it shall be forgiven....
Go, and sin.... No more.

The stars eddy, swallowed in a whirlwind.
Yet from this black sky, not snow —
the manna of God's irony. Instead,
petals falling: frail white shells
small as a grain of sand.
As a nascent hope.

Bethlehem

Jog-sweat streaking down her back,
under the hot sling of the halter top,
she pauses where she never has before,
at the black canopy of pine and oak that shields
Bethlehem Cemetery, Established 1845,
from her century.
                    The morning air heavy
as the overnight news, the only sound
the tinny *critch-critch* of a drum set riffing
through the earbuds she's looped across
her shoulder. Until she cuts her iPod off,
floats free of its slim white tether, the bark
she sails in swinging under the black canopy
and out, into the narrow channel
of this dusty Styx.
                    Tottering slabs, broken slabs
of limestone. Of slate. And granite. The uniform
ones, the ones at careful intervals, mark families,
some as nameless as the prehistoric dead,
two names prominent after all those many years.
And she thinks, *even in the graveyard folks still try*
to make a name for themselves. Here, bounded in marble,
are the Cunninghams, there the Jacksons,
1892 a hard year for the Cunninghams.

Four plain stones mark four children gone,
two in that awful year alone. In the Jackson plot,
a single marker for a double loss: *Twin Daughters*
Born and Died June 13.
                    From her silent bark,

she watches the silent Cunninghams and Jacksons,
corseted, frock-coated, black-draped to the ankles.
They stand where mother and father sleep
their sleep, *Gone but not forgotten. At rest with Jesus
now,* and listen to the hopeful words, to the hollow
drumming of tossed earth, as earth meets earth....

She floats back under the canopy, past
the dissolving headstones, the anemic Our Lord's
candles, the ice-white destroying angels
feasting on the hewn logs that circle Bethlehem
like ancient city limit signs. Back into the hot sun
and smog, where clocks still tick off
the century. She feels her runner's heart
finally wound down to this dull,
this miraculous quotidian pace.
Feels the descent of the tiny replication
of herself that has been waiting for its time
since before all worlds.

Selective Memory

Old Faithful wasn't really faithful hour
on the hour. And I didn't even know
what a Liberty Cap was until Delacroix
showed me—though it took me decades
to get past Mademoiselle Liberté's white
wicked knockers, to her "Phrygian" headgear.

No, much more vividly I remember paint pots
spitting out their liquid quids of clay: detritus
from an errant potter's potter's wheel,
"paint" the universal hue of whole wheat dough.
Benign. Unless a hot blob got on you, mating
with your skin like a cancer. The fumaroles hissed
and pissed *their* way into memory—muddy cats
in heat, their backs up. They would have taken
the skin off in an instant with one wrong step,
gone down to bone in the shortest of short order.

A place of gorgeous "what-if?" danger is what
I recall: Crazy shutterbugs forgoing the safety
of their cars for shots of blasé bison champing
weeds. A slammed door could have spooked
them into 900 pounds per head of galumphing terror.
It didn't happen. But while we visited—Mom,
Dad, and eighth-grade I—a bear on the prowl
for ursine fast food got into a tent, gnawed
the heads of two sleep-dazzled campers
to the skull. A third got away, *I only
have escaped alone to tell thee of it....*

Nature can't be loved too freely; it doesn't
love you back. That's the moral of the tale
that I draw now. And yet for me, Yellowstone
is much more memorably the manmade story
of an old cold hotel without TV. So poorly run
by the Park Service that in a seedy CCC-built
dining hall-cum-movie house out back,
they were showing, this spring of '62, a 1940s
Cary Grant flick in smudged black-and-white.
A soundtrack like some underwater tête-à-tête.

Afterwards, we went back to our Spartan little room,
down nighted corridors. Gray walls and three small
iron beds all in row, with high arched heads,
Like we're the Three Bears! I recall Mom saying:
How can anything so niggling and pathetic
now appear "just right"

in the strobe-lit halls of memory?

Kite Flying at Brigantine

For Lew

We loft our red box kite in sky so clear,
sun-bleached, it's livid, like a hurt—rope burn,
a knee skinned down to dermis.... (Now I spurn
the "great outdoors," though once I didn't fear
de rigueur summer ills....) Kite's paid out near
a thousand feet seaward, only to yearn
for more. You race down to the store, return
with one last spool. It's harder yet to steer!

In fresh-gale winds, ardor unsatisfied,
the thing breaks loose, and learns that freedom's good.
We've lost our kite! Still, that's all right with us.
We stare till our eyes burn, until kite's plied
its higher course above the sea, red dust
speck where bold swaths, broad as a flag, once stood.

The Needlefish

An iridescent streamer, dill-green, dill-
leaflike, swings from the pilings. While he feeds,
the underbelly shows, translucent as the flesh
of pickles left in brine too long, down to the waxy
aureoles of seeds in rows. The jaws' tensile probe
samples an unseen growth there against the wood.
Green fades to brown, cinema style. Melts briefly
into the shadow of the pier, then returns, now in school:
a flight of watery parrots squeezed and condensed
under the lens of the surface
to syringes, to thirsty vacuums that drag
the bay's wet wealth through bodies thin as glass,
mottled with graduations
millimeter-true — instruments
precise as anyone could make them.

Wild Turkeys near Robertstown

For Donna

You said these birds were gun-shy; like a clutch
of dark-robed monks in conclave, they would never
come this near the road—leave woods' deep thatch,
the underbrush of fields and swamps—or ever

risk the white dry grass along the shoulder,
where they're blatant as a text hand-sewn
into a tapestry—a species bolder
than their mythic brethren, unicorns! Flown

their cloister in the woods, right here beside
the road are six, or maybe eight, arranged
in perfect cleric file, their feathers dyed
that oak-leaf brown they turn with season's change.

A wonder, then, in these gray wastes, the wind
a knife that winter holds against the chin....

Instinct

They're known as *nimbostratus,*
these clouds that look as if drawn
with a straightedge: gray ledge
of rock. A dirty waterfall of rain

sheers from them. All around,
the sweaty air moils; tree leaves
swim, seething and sinuating
through rapids, exposing the quick-

silver of their ribs, their undersides.
Equivocal birds zigzag down
current, fumbling in a whorl
of leaf tatters, feeling their way

toward the never-before-
seen shoals called *home.*

Sight-Reading Schumann's "The Prophet Bird"

Against a sky as slatey as the topside
of a pool table, the robin sits her crooked
mast of yaupon holly like an Ishmael

contemplating the infinite ocean of the self.
Her beak set toward the gale known as *March,*
she rides her nest as if she'd fight you

for each millimeter's weave of pine straw,
leaf scrap, looking out to the horizon
of her own small soul. To that avian

equal of the thousand-eyed Krishna.
Or the white-hot Christ transmogrified,
flying the image of Elijah like an ensign

in the blue over Palestine. She devours
her avian edition of the I Ching, the Torah,
the Koran. Tells her rosary again and again,

each fat blue bead.

§

Notes

Poetry and Murder: The city mentioned in this poem is Altoona, Pennsylvania. Wopsononock Mountain, about six miles from downtown, provides a spectacular lookout.

Dia de los Muertos: This poem mentions several of the ritual elements important on the Day of the Dead, which is celebrated in Latin American countries on November 1 (All Saints' Day). The ceremonial gruel and bread are set out to entertain the spirits of ancestors who are presumed to visit that day. *Petates* are bedrolls put down for the visiting dead to rest themselves on.

Two Tales Told Out of School: Teaching, especially in college, introduced me to remarkable ways of reading and thinking about literature. Actually, most instructors are probably fairly staid in their way of looking at literature. But contemporary students come at literature from a position that is mostly untroubled by traditional methods of explication and, indeed, without any of the accepted language of critical analysis that is the lingua franca of academics. For example, even gifted students have little clue that academe requires formal, not to say (oh, hell, maybe we can say it here!) stilted, diction. That can lead to fresh but amusing approaches to literature.

Listening to my students dissect literary works, I tried to imagine how a reasonably intelligent and articulate student of the type I describe above might retell stories that appear in Western literary classics. Of the two included here, the story from Genesis is well known and available to most readers. Since Dante Gabriel Rossetti's free translation of Gottfried Bürger's "Lenore" is less familiar (even though Bürger's original was a watershed work in European Romanticism), I include the text below. It's corny as hell but otherwise a pretty good piece of writing for one as young as Rossetti was when he penned it (sixteen). In fact, it's the earliest poem he allowed to appear in his collected works.

By the way, it's probably best not to try to figure out Rossetti's historical references in the poem. One conjecture is that "King Frederick" is Frederick II of Prussia, who waged war (the Second Silesian War) on Prague in 1744. That would make the "Empress" mentioned in the poem Maria Theresa of Austria. Most translators before Rossetti, including

Walter Taylor and Sir Walter Scott in English, give the poem a medieval setting. As far as I can tell, Rossetti throws in the reference to Hungary for its exotic (at least to the sixteen-year-old Rossetti) resonances.

Lenore

Trans. Dante Gabriel Rossetti

Up rose Lenore as the red morn wore,
    From weary visions starting;
"Art faithless, William, or, William, art dead?
    'Tis long since thy departing."
For he, with Frederick's men of might,
In fair Prague waged the uncertain fight;
Nor once had he writ in the hurry of war,
And sad was the true heart that sickened afar.

The Empress and the King,
    With ceaseless quarrel tired,
At length relaxed the stubborn hate
    Which rivalry inspired:
And the martial throng, with laugh and song,
Spoke of their homes as they rode along,
And clank, clank, clank! came every rank,
With the trumpet-sound that rose and sank.

And here and there and everywhere,
    Along the swarming ways,
Went old man and boy, with music of joy,
    On the gallant bands to gaze;
And the young child shouted to spy the vaward,
And trembling and blushing the bride pressed forward:
But ah! for the sweet lips of Lenore
The kiss and the greeting are vanished and o'er.

From man to man all wildly she ran
    With a swift and searching eye;
But she felt alone in the mighty mass,
    As it crushed and crowded by:
On hurried the troop,—a gladsome group,—
And proudly the tall plumes wave and droop:
She tore her hair and she turned her round,
And madly she dashed her against the ground.

Her mother clasped her tenderly
    With soothing words and mild:
"My child, may God look down on thee,—
    God comfort thee, my child."
"Oh! mother, mother! gone is gone!
I reck no more how the world runs on:
What pity to me does God impart?
Woe, woe, woe! for my heavy heart!"

"Help, Heaven, help and favour her!
    Child, utter an Ave Marie!
Wise and great are the doings of God;
    He loves and pities thee."
"Out, mother, out, on the empty lie!
Doth he heed my despair,—doth he list to my cry?
What boots it now to hope or to pray?
The night is come,—there is no more day."

"Help, Heaven, help! who knows the Father
    Knows surely that he loves his child:
The bread and the wine from the hand divine
    Shall make thy tempered grief less wild."
"Oh! mother, dear mother! the wine and the bread
Will not soften the anguish that bows down my head;
For bread and for wine it will yet be as late
That his cold corpse creeps from the grim grave's gate."

"What if the traitor's false faith failed,
    By sweet temptation tried,—
What if in distant Hungary
    He clasp another bride?—
Despise the fickle fool, my girl,
Who hath ta'en the pebble and spurned the pearl:
While soul and body shall hold together
In his perjured heart shall be stormy weather."

"Oh! mother, mother! gone is gone,
    And lost will still be lost!
Death, death is the goal of my weary soul,
    Crushed and broken and crost.
Spark of my life! down, down to the tomb:
Die away in the night, die away in the gloom!
What pity to me does God impart?
Woe, woe, woe! for my heavy heart!"

"Help, Heaven, help, and heed her not,
    For her sorrows are strong within;
She knows not the words that her tongue repeats,—
    Oh! Count them not for sin!
Cease, cease, my child, thy wretchedness,
And think on the promised happiness;
So shall thy mind's calm ecstasy
Be a hope and a home and a bridegroom to thee."

"My mother, what is happiness?
    My mother, what is Hell?
With William is my happiness,—
    Without him is my Hell!
Spark of my life! down, down to the tomb:
Die away in the night, die away in the gloom!
Earth and Heaven, Heaven and earth,
Reft of William are nothing worth."

Thus grief racked and tore the breast of Lenore,
    And was busy at her brain;
Thus rose her cry to the Power on high,
    To question and arraign:
Wringing her hands and beating her breast,—
Tossing and rocking without any rest;—
Till from her light veil the moon shone thro',
And the stars leapt out on the darkling blue.

But hark to the clatter and the pat pat patter!
    Of a horse's heavy hoof!
How the steel clanks and rings as the rider springs!
    How the echo shouts aloof!
While silently and lightly the gentle bell
Tingles and jingles softly and well;
And low and clear through the door plank thin
Comes the voice without to the ear within:

"Holla! holla! unlock the gate;
    Art waking, my bride, or sleeping?
Is thy heart still free and faithful to me?
    Art laughing, my bride, or weeping?"
"Oh! wearily, William, I've waited for you,—
Woefully watching the long day thro',—
With a great sorrow sorrowing
For the cruelty of your tarrying."

"Till the dead midnight we saddled not,—
    I have journeyed far and fast—
And hither I come to carry thee back
    Ere the darkness shall be past."
"Ah! rest thee within till the night's more calm;
Smooth shall thy couch be, and soft, and warm:
Hark to winds, how they whistle and rush
Thro' the twisted twine of the hawthorn-bush."

"Thro' the hawthorn-bush let whistle and rush,—
    Let whistle, child, let whistle!
Mark the flash fierce and high of my steed's bright eye,
    And his proud crest's eager bristle.
Up, up and away! I must not stay:
Mount swiftly behind me! up, up and away!
An hundred miles must be ridden and sped
Ere we may lie down in the bridal-bed."

"What! ride an hundred miles to-night,
    By thy mad fancies driven!
Dost hear the bell with its sullen swell,
    As it rumbles out eleven?"
"Look forth! look forth! the moon shines bright:
We and the dead gallop fast thro' the night.
'Tis for a wager I bear thee away
To the nuptial couch ere break of day."

"Ah! where is the chamber, William dear,
    And William, where is the bed?"
"Far, far from here: still, narrow, and cool:
    Plank and bottom and lid."
"Hast room for me?"—"For me and thee;
Up, up to the saddle right speedily!
The wedding-guests are gathered and met,
And the door of the chamber is open set."

She busked her well, and into the selle
    She sprang with nimble haste,—
And gently smiling, with a sweet beguiling,
    Her white hands clasped his waist:—
And hurry, hurry! ring, ring, ring!
To and fro they sway and swing;
Snorting and snuffing they skim the ground,
And the sparks fly up, and the stones run round.

Here to the right and there to the left
    Flew fields of corn and clover,
And the bridges flashed by to the dazzled eye,
    As rattling they thundered over.
"What ails my love? the moon shines bright:
Bravely the dead men ride through the night.
Is my love afraid of the quiet dead?"
"Ah! no; — let them sleep in their dusty bed!"

On the breeze cool and soft what tune floats aloft,
    While the crows wheel overhead? —
Ding dong! ding dong! 'tis the sound, 'tis the song, —
    "Room, room for the passing dead!"
Slowly the funeral-train drew near,
Bearing the coffin, bearing the bier;
And the chime of their chant was hissing and harsh,
Like the note of the bull-frog within the marsh.

"You bury your corpse at the dark midnight,
    With hymns and bells and wailing; —
But I bring home my youthful wife
    To a bride-feast's rich regaling.
Come, chorister, come with thy choral throng,
And solemnly sing me a marriage-song;
Come, friar, come, — let the blessing be spoken,
That the bride and the bridegroom's sweet rest be unbroken."

Died the dirge and vanished the bier: —
    Obedient to his call,
Hard hard behind, with a rush like the wind,
    Came the long steps' pattering fall:
And ever further! ring, ring, ring!
To and fro they sway and swing;
Snorting and snuffing they skim the ground,
And the sparks spurt up, and the stones run round.

How flew to the right, how flew to the left,
    Trees, mountains in the race!
How to the left, and the right and the left,
    Flew town and market-place!
"What ails my love? the moon shines bright:
Bravely the dead men ride thro' the night.
Is my love afraid of the quiet dead?"
"Ah! let them alone in their dusty bed!"

See, see, see! by the gallows-tree,
    As they dance on the wheel's broad hoop,
Up and down, in the gleam of the moon
    Half lost, an airy group: —
"Ho, ho! mad mob, come hither amain,
And join in the wake of my rushing train; —
Come, dance me a dance, ye dancers thin,
Ere the planks of the marriage bed close us in."

And hush, hush, hush! the dreamy rout
    Came close with a ghastly bustle,
Like the whirlwind in the hazel-bush,
    When it makes the dry leaves rustle:
And faster, faster! ring, ring, ring!
To and fro they sway and swing;
Snorting and snuffing they skim the ground,
And the sparks spurt up, and the stones run round.

How flew the moon high overhead,
    In the wild race madly driven!
In and out, how the stars danced about,
    And reeled o'er the flashing heaven!
"What ails my love? the moon shines bright:
Bravely the dead men ride thro' the night.
Is my love afraid of the quiet dead?"
"Alas! let them alone in their dusty bed!"

"Horse, horse! meseems 'tis the cock's shrill note,
    And the sand is well nigh spent; —
Horse, horse, away! 'tis the break of day,
    'Tis the morning air's sweet scent.
Finished, finished is our ride:
Room, room for the bridegroom and the bride!
At last, at last, we have reached the spot,
For the speed of the dead man has slackened not!"

And swiftly up to an iron gate
    With reins relaxed they went;
At the rider's touch the bolts flew back,
    And the bars were broken and bent;
The doors were burst with a deafening knell,
And over the white graves they dashed pell mell:
The tombs around looked grassy and grim,
As they glimmered and glanced in the moonlight dim.

> But see! But see! in an eyelid's beat,
>   Towhoo! a ghastly wonder!
> The horseman's jerkin, piece by piece,
>   Dropped off like brittle tinder!
> Fleshless and hairless, a naked skull,
> The sight of his weird head was horrible;
> The lifelike mask was there no more,
> And a scythe and a sandglass the skeleton bore.
>
> Loud snorted the horse as he plunged and reared,
>   And the sparks were scattered round: —
> What man shall say if he vanished away,
>   Or sank in the gaping ground?
> Groans from the earth and shrieks in the air!
> Howling and wailing everywhere!
> Half dead, half living, the soul of Lenore
> Fought as it never had fought before.
>
> The churchyard troop, — a ghostly group, —
>   Close round the dying girl;
> Out and in they hurry and spin
>   Through the dancer's weary whirl:
> "Patience, patience, when the heart is breaking;
> With thy God there is no question-making:
> Of thy body thou art quit and free:
> Heaven keep thy soul eternally!"

Too Much: This poem refers to one of William Wordsworth's sonnets:

> The world is too much with us; late and soon,
> Getting and spending, we lay waste our powers;
> Little we see in Nature that is ours;
> We have given our hearts away, a sordid boon!
> This Sea that bares her bosom to the moon,
> The winds that will be howling at all hours,
> And are up-gathered now like sleeping flowers,
> For this, for everything, we are out of tune;
> It moves us not. — Great God! I'd rather be
> A Pagan suckled in a creed outworn;
> So might I, standing on this pleasant lea,
> Have glimpses that would make me less forlorn;
> Have sight of Proteus rising from the sea;
> Or hear old Triton blow his wreathed horn.

Dante's Confession: Dante's "famous swoon" over the fate of Paolo and Francesca is often interpreted as the poet's inability to see things from God's perspective: in pitying, he fails to understand that God's justice is behind eternal punishment.

Requiescat: Oscar Wilde spent two years in prison following his conviction for gross indecency, the upshot of a love affair with Lord Alfred Douglas. Douglas's father, the Marquess of Queensbury (the same gent responsible for the rules of modern boxing), brought the charges that put Wilde away. After release in 1897, the writer lived the remaining three years of his life in impoverished exile in Paris, reliant on the "kindness of strangers," especially expatriate Britons. Reportedly, while savoring a glass of champagne on his deathbed, Wilde quipped, "Alas, I am dying beyond my means." He expired at L'Hôtel D'Alsace (a presumptive fleabag) in 1900.

Pilate's Epistle to the Romans: The *Emperor* is Tiberius. Pilate was deposed by Lucius Vitellius the Elder, governor of Syria under Tiberius. The time and cause of Pilate's death is not known for sure, though some traditions hold that he was banished to Gaul, where he took his own life.

Selective Memory: Eugène Delacroix's 1830 painting *Liberty Leading the People* features Liberty anthropomorphized as a young woman, breasts exposed, leading the armed populace of Paris during the French Revolution. Liberty carries the tricolor flag of the Revolution; on her head is a conical liberty cap, also called a Phrygian cap. The Liberty Cap geyser in Yellowstone National Park is so called because it vented from a similarly shaped cap of stone called geyserite rising forty-five feet from the earth. The geyser is now extinct.

The Needlefish: *Strongylura marina,* common name *Atlantic needlefish,* plies the waters between Maine and Brazil. As the name implies, it is a very strung-out little fish (averaging around a foot in length), with a long, long jaw filled with many tiny teeth.

Sight Reading Schumann's "The Prophet Bird": One of nine short piano pieces in Robert Schumann's 1848 collection *Waldscenen* (*Forest Scenes*). "The Prophet Bird" (German: *"Vogel als Prophet"*) is the most famous, considered a forerunner of musical Impressionism, which came into its own almost fifty years later. It's spooky but quite beautiful.

Acknowledgments

The poems in this volume first appeared in the following publications, sometimes in different versions:

Ambit: "L'art pour l'art"; *Apalachee Quarterly*: "A Matter of Perspective (II)"; *Avocet*: "My Churchyard"; *Blue Fifth Review*: "Jardin des Muses"; *Chattahoochee Review*: "Heaven"; *Chiron Review*: "Brass Rubbing," "Dia de los Muertos"; *Cider Press Review*: "Cloudscape with Heron"; *Chaffin Journal*: "Civil Rights"; *Concho River Review*: "Pilate's Epistle to the Romans"; *Ekphrasis*: "Rara Avis"; *FutureCycle Poetry*: "Instinct"; *Green Fuse*: "The Needlefish"; *Iodine Poetry Journal*: "All Global Warming Is Local"; *Kennesaw Review*: "Wild Turkeys near Robertstown"; *The Lowell Pearl*: "Poetry and Murder"; *The Melic Review*: "Relativity Theory," "Too Much"; *Möbius*: "Memorial"; *The New Formalist*: "Kite Flying at Brigantine"; *Numinous Magazine*: "In the Screening Room"; *The Other Journal*: "There's a Divinity"; *Poems & Plays*: "Augury"; *Poetrybay*: "Memento Mori"; *Right Hand Pointing*: "Old Husbands' Tale"; *Salt River Review*: "Dante's Confession"; *ShatterColors Literary Review*: "Requiescat"; *Stickman Review*: "Bethlehem"; *Terrain.org*: "Call of the Wild"; *Ship of Fools*: "Cold Snap, Ides of March"; *Umbrella*: "Pavlov's, Down by the Log Dump," "Selective Memory"; *Ygdrasil*: "Beasts in Their Jungles," "From The Book of the Dead," "Psalm," "Sight-Reading Schumann's 'The Prophet Bird,'" "The Truth about Myths"

"Living in the Museum" first appeared in the anthology *Out of A/Maze* (Chiron Review Press, 1996).

Cover art, 1973 photograph by Tom Hubbard of "D'aug Days" dance performance in Cincinnati, Ohio (U.S. National Archives 412-DA-10802); cover and interior book design by Diane Kistner (dkistner@futurecycle.org); Book Antiqua text and Cronos Pro titling

About FutureCycle Press

FutureCycle Press is dedicated to publishing lasting English-language poetry books, chapbooks, and anthologies in both print-on-demand and ebook formats. Founded in 2007 by long-time independent editor/publishers and partners Diane Kistner and Robert S. King, the press incorporated as a nonprofit in 2012. A number of our editors are distinguished poets and writers in their own right, and we have been actively involved in the small press movement going back to the early seventies.

The FutureCycle Poetry Book Prize and honorarium is awarded annually for the best full-length volume of poetry we publish in a calendar year. Introduced in 2013, our Good Works projects are devoted to issues of universal significance, with all proceeds donated to a related worthy cause. Our Selected Poems series highlights contemporary poets with a substantial body of work to their credit.

We are dedicated to giving all of the authors we publish the care their work deserves, making our catalog of titles the most diverse and distinguished it can be, and paying forward any earnings to fund more great books.

We've learned a few things about independent publishing over the years. We've also evolved a unique, resilient publishing model that allows us to focus mainly on vetting and preserving for posterity the most books of exceptional quality without becoming overwhelmed with bookkeeping and mailing, fundraising activities, or taxing editorial and production "bubbles." To find out more about what we are doing, come see us at www.futurecycle.org.

Made in the USA
Charleston, SC
24 January 2014